Questions and Answers: Countries

Pakistan

A Question and Answer Book

by Gillia M. Olson

Consultant:
Keith Snodgrass
South Asia Center, Outreach Coordinator and Associate Director
University of Washington
Seattle, Washington

Capstone
press

Mankato, Minnesota

Fact Finders is published by Capstone Press,
151 Good Counsel Drive, P.O. Box 669, Mankato, Minnesota 56002.
www.capstonepress.com

Library of Congress Cataloging-in-Publication Data
Olson, Gillia M.
    Pakistan: A question and answer book / by Gillia M. Olson.
    p. cm.—(Fact finders. Questions and answers. Countries)
    Includes bibliographical references and index.
    ISBN 0-7368-3757-4 (hardcover)
    1. Pakistan—Juvenile literature. I. Title. II. Series.
DS376.9.O45 2005
954.91—dc22   2004010805

Summary: Describes the geography, history, economy, and culture of Pakistan in a
    question-and-answer format.

Editorial Credits
Megan Schoeneberger, editor; Kia Adams, set designer; Kate Opseth, book designer; Nancy
    Steers, map illustrator; Wanda Winch, photo researcher; Scott Thoms, photo editor

Photo Credits
Alamy/Cephas Picture Library, 25
Art Directors/M. Barlow, 10–11; TRIP, 1, 21
Atlas/Gunes Kocatepe, 17; Ugur Uluocak, 4
Coral Planet/Nasuh Mahruki, 13
Corbis/Ed Kashi, 14–15, 19; Galen Rowell, 27; Keren Su, cover (foreground); Nik Wheeler, 12;
    Reuters, 23
Corel, cover (background)
Getty Images Inc./AFP/Press Information Department, 9; Keystone/Douglas Miller, 7
Photo courtesy of Paul Baker, 29 (coins)
Photo courtesy of Ron Wise, 29 (bill)
StockHaus Ltd., 29 (flag)

1 2 3 4 5 6 10 09 08 07 06 05

Table of Contents

Features

Where is Pakistan?

Pakistan is in southern Asia. It is nearly twice the size of California.

Mountains cover much of Pakistan. The Hindu Kush Mountains border Afghanistan. The Karakoram Range in northern Pakistan is home to the world's second tallest mountain, K2. The Himalaya mountain range crosses northern Pakistan and into India.

The snowy peak of K2 reaches above the clouds. ➤

The Indus River divides the country. To the east are rolling plains. Farmers use water from the Indus to grow crops there. West of the Indus lies the dry, rocky Baluchistan **Plateau**.

When did Pakistan become a country?

Pakistan became a country in August 1947. At that time, the United Kingdom gave up control of much of southern Asia. Two countries were formed, India and Pakistan. Mohammed Ali Jinnah led Pakistan's struggle for independence.

Pakistan and India are separate countries because of religion. Pakistan became a home for Muslims. They follow **Islam**. India became a home for Hindus, Muslims, and others.

Fact!

Pakistan means "Land of the Pure" in Urdu. Urdu is one of Pakistan's official languages.

Mohammed Ali Jinnah (center) met with other world leaders in 1946 to plan Pakistan's independence.

India and Pakistan still fight over an area called Jammu and Kashmir. The land area lies between the two countries, near northeast Pakistan.

What type of government does Pakistan have?

Pakistan is a **federation** of four **provinces** and three territories. Like U.S. states, each province has its own government.

Like the U.S. Congress, Pakistan's national **legislature** has two parts. They are called the National Assembly and the Senate. The National Assembly has 342 members. They serve 5-year terms. The Senate has 100 members who serve 6-year terms.

Fact!

Sixty seats in the National Assembly are set aside for women. Ten seats are set aside for non-Muslims.

Pakistan's prime minister (standing) speaks to the National Assembly in 2003.

The leader of the largest political party in the legislature becomes the **prime minister**. This person leads the legislature. He or she also leads the **cabinet** that works with the president. The president is Pakistan's head of state.

What kind of housing does Pakistan have?

Most Pakistanis live in homes with only one or two rooms. Pakistanis with more money live in larger houses. Houses and apartment buildings in cities are often made of cement. They have cement, wood, or metal roofs. In rural areas, most houses are made of mud bricks.

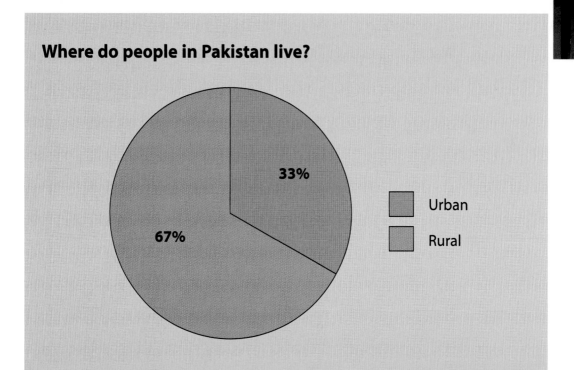

Where do people in Pakistan live?

33%

67%

Urban

Rural

Some rural homes have modern conveniences, such as satellite dishes.

Most homes have electricity but not other services. Many homes have no running water. People get water from nearby wells. Most areas do not have underground **sewers** or garbage collection.

What are Pakistan's forms of transportation?

Pakistanis in cities often ride buses, taxis, and bicycles. Most people in rural areas use pack animals, buses, and tractors to get around. Most Pakistanis do not own cars.

Pakistan uses ships to carry goods. Pakistan's location on the Arabian Sea is important for trade. Karachi is the main port. Goods come into and leave Karachi by ship.

Ships carry goods to Port Qasim in Karachi. ➤

Drivers wait by their colorful buses to carry passengers in Islamabad.

Trains and airplanes are used to carry goods and people long distances. Railroads connect large cities. Many cities also have airports. Pakistan's main airport is in Karachi.

What are Pakistan's major industries?

Nearly half of all Pakistanis work in fishing or farming **industries**. Pakistani fishers catch shrimp, sardines, and sharks in the Arabian Sea. Farmers grow wheat and rice to eat or to sell at markets.

Farm products are used in Pakistan's factories. Farmers sell cotton and food to factories. Factories make the cotton into **textiles** and process the food. They then sell the textiles and food to other countries.

What does Pakistan import and export?	
Imports	**Exports**
chemicals	cotton and cotton textiles
machinery	rice
petroleum	leather goods

Workers prepare cotton for a factory in eastern Pakistan.

Services make up a large group of jobs in Pakistan. Many people work as cooks and maids in other people's homes. Teaching, health care, and banking are also important services in Pakistan.

What is school like in Pakistan?

Pakistan's government does not require children to go to school. Many parents cannot pay for school. Only about half of children ages 5 to 10 attend school. More boys go to school than girls.

Children who do go to school begin in elementary school. When they are 10 years old, they start middle school. After three years, they move on to secondary school.

Fact!

Pakistan's school year lasts from September to June. Students get a break in July and August.

Secondary school lasts two years. Students then choose between two types of higher secondary schools. Each lasts two more years. Technical schools give job training. Other schools prepare students for colleges and universities.

What are Pakistan's favorite sports and games?

Pakistani men play *kabaddi*, a traditional Pakistani sport. In this game, two teams each take a side of a playing field. One player, the raider, runs across the center line. He then tries to touch as many players as possible. The raider tries to return to his side of the field. The other team's players try to stop him. They wrestle the raider and hold him down. If the raider is able to return, his team scores. If he doesn't make it back, the other team scores.

Fact!

A kabaddi raider cannot take a breath for 30 seconds while he chases the other team. He must return to his side before the 30 seconds are over.

A kabaddi raider tries to run past the other team.

Pakistanis also play soccer, polo, field hockey, and other sports. Squash and cricket are two favorite sports in Pakistan. They came from the United Kingdom. Squash is like racquetball. Cricket is like baseball.

What are the traditional art forms in Pakistan?

Poetry and music are traditional art forms in Pakistan. *Mushaira* are poetry readings in large groups. *Ghazals* are Islamic poems that are often sung. *Qawwali* is a type of music. *Qawwali* musicians sing Islamic songs about peace and love. The songs sometimes cause listeners to go into a sleeplike trance.

Fact!

Qawwali *singer Nusrat Fateh Ali Khan made 125 albums during his lifetime, more than any other* Qawwali *singer.*

A Pakistani carpet maker weaves a rug with colorful designs.

Many Pakistanis make art for a living. Some artists make and sell bronze plates and bowls with detailed designs. Carpet makers weave designs into rugs. Pakistani carpets are sold throughout the world. Other artists make pottery or sew designs onto cloth.

What major holidays do people in Pakistan celebrate?

Most Pakistanis celebrate Islamic holidays. Ramadan is a month in which people **fast** from sunrise to sundown. At the end of the month, people celebrate with a feast called Eid al-Fitr.

Eid al-Adha is the Islamic feast of the sacrifice. It honors Abraham's willingness to give up his son to God. God allowed him to kill a ram instead of his son. Some people honor the holiday by killing a ram. They give some of the meat to the poor.

What other holidays do people in Pakistan celebrate?

Birthday of the prophet Muhammad
Commemoration of Jinnah's death
International Labor Day
Mohammed Ali Jinnah's birthday

Young people gather to sing in celebration of Independence Day.

Pakistanis have two holidays to celebrate when Pakistan became a country. Pakistan Day is held on March 23. It honors the day Muslim leaders decided to form a Muslim nation. August 14 is Pakistan's Independence Day.

What are the traditional foods of Pakistan?

Most Pakistani meals include wheat or rice. Chapati is a popular flat bread made from wheat. Rice is often mixed with meat and vegetables as a main dish. Common meats are lamb, beef, and chicken. Spices are often used to flavor rice dishes. Rice is also used with milk to make a pudding dessert.

Fact!

The Islamic religion does not allow Muslims to eat pork or drink alcohol.

A group of Muslim men eat a meal of bread, meat, and rice.

Common drinks include milk, juices, and tea. Pakistanis drink milk from goats, cows, and water buffalo. *Lassi* is a creamy yogurt drink. Pakistanis squeeze melons, apples, pomegranates, and mangoes into juices.

What is family life like in Pakistan?

A day in Pakistan starts with prayer. At dawn, a religious leader calls Muslims to prayer. The prayer is the first of five throughout the day.

After breakfast, men go to work. Many women also work. Some children go to school. Others do chores or work for their family.

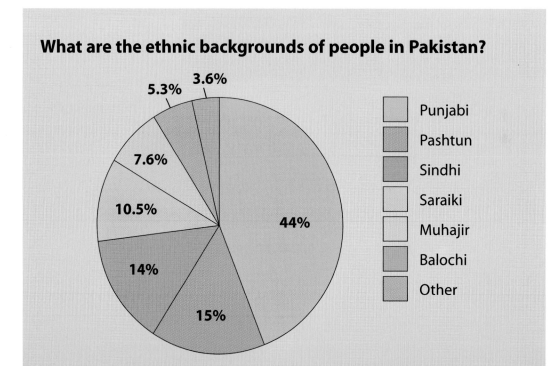

What are the ethnic backgrounds of people in Pakistan?

- Punjabi
- Pashtun
- Sindhi
- Saraiki
- Muhajir
- Balochi
- Other

3.6%
5.3%
7.6%
10.5%
14%
15%
44%

Rural Pakistani families often do not have furniture in their homes. They sit on the floor.

Hospitality is an important part of Pakistani culture. Guests are often given the best food and drink. Overnight guests usually receive the best room or bed. Pakistanis want to make everyone feel welcome.

Pakistan Fast Facts

Official name:

Islamic Republic of Pakistan

Land area:

*310,402 square miles
(803,940 square kilometers)*

**Average annual
precipitation:**

10 inches (25.4 centimeters)

**Average January
temperature (Islamabad):**

*50 degrees Fahrenheit
(10 degrees Celsius)*

**Average July temperature
(Islamabad):**

*85 degrees Fahrenheit
(29 degrees Celsius)*

Population:

150,694,740 people

Capital city:

Islamabad

Languages:

Urdu, English

Natural resources:

*bauxite, copper, low-grade coal,
natural gas*

Religions:

Islamic	*97%*
Christian, Hindu, and other	*3%*

Money and Flag

Money:

Pakistan's money is called the Pakistani rupee. In 2004, 1 U.S. dollar equaled 57.4 rupees. One Canadian dollar equaled 41.7 rupees.

Flag:

Pakistan's flag is green with a vertical white stripe. A white crescent moon and star lie in the green area. They are traditional symbols of Islam.

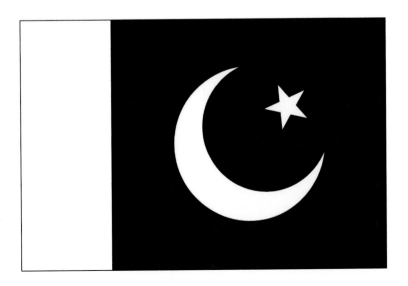

Learn to Speak Urdu

Many people in Pakistan speak Urdu. It is one of Pakistan's official languages. Learn to speak some Urdu using the words below.

English	Urdu	Pronunciation
hello	assalam-o-alaikum	(UH-soo-lam-OH-UH-layk-um)
good-bye	khuda-hafiz	(koo-da-ha-FEZ)
please	khush karna	(KOOSH KAR-na)
thank you	shukria	(shoo-KREE-uh)

Glossary

cabinet (KAB-in-it)—a group of advisors for the head of a country

fast (FAST)—to give up eating for a period of time

federation (fed-uh-RAY-shuhn)—a union of states, provinces, or territories

hospitality (hoss-puh-TAL-uh-tee)—a generous and friendly way of treating people, especially guests, so that they feel comfortable

industry (IN-duh-stree)—a single branch of business or trade

Islam (ISS-luhm)—the religion based on the teachings of Muhammad; Muslims believe that Allah is God and that Muhammad is Allah's prophet; Islam's holy book is the Koran.

legislature (LEJ-iss-lay-chur)—a group of people that has the power to make or change laws for a state or country

plateau (pla-TOH)—an area of high, flat land

prime minister (PRIME MIN-uh-stur)—the person in charge of a government in some countries

province (PROV-uhnss)—a district or a region of some countries

sewer (SOO-ur)—a system, often an underground pipe, that carries away liquid and solid waste

textile (TEK-stile)—fabric or cloth that has been woven or knitted

Internet Sites

FactHound offers a safe, fun way to find Internet sites related to this book.
All of the sites on FactHound have been researched by our staff.

Here's how:
1. Visit *www.facthound.com*
2. Type in this special code **0736837574**
   for age-appropriate sites. Or enter a
   search word related to this book for
   a more general search.
3. Click on the **Fetch It** button.

FactHound will fetch the best sites for you!

Read More

DeAngelis, Gina. *Pakistan.* Many Cultures, One World. Mankato,
Minn.: Blue Earth Books, 2004.

Sharth, Sharon. *Pakistan.* Faces and Places. Chanhassen, Minn.: Child's
World, 2003.

Walsh, Kieran. *Pakistan.* Countries in the News. Vero Beach, Fla.:
Rourke, 2004.

Index